better together*

*This book is best read together, grownup and kid.

 akidsco.com

a
kids
book
about

a kids book about about

Strength

by Sam Johnson

A Kids Co.
Editors Jennifer Goldstein and Emma Wolf
Designer Rick DeLucco
Creative Director Rick DeLucco
Studio Manager Kenya Feldes
Sales Director Melanie Wilkins
Head of Books Jennifer Goldstein
CEO and Founder Jelani Memory

DK
Delhi Technical Team Bimlesh Tiwary Pushpak Tyagi, Rakesh Kumar
Senior Production Editor Jennifer Murray
Senior Production Controller Louise Minihane
Senior Acquisitions Editor Katy Flint
Acquisitions Project Editor Sara Forster
Managing Art Editor Vicky Short
Managing Director, Licensing Mark Searle

First American edition, 2025
Published in the United States by DK Publishing, 1745 Broadway, 20th Floor,
New York, NY 10019

First published in Great Britain in 2025 by
Dorling Kindersley Limited, 20 Vauxhall Bridge Road, London SW1V 2SA
A Penguin Random House Company

The authorised representative in the EEA is
Dorling Kindersley Verlag GmbH. Arnulfstr. 124, 80636 Munich, Germany

A catalog record for this book is available from the Library of Congress.
A CIP catalogue record for this book is available from the British Library.
ISBN: 978-0-2417-4386-7

DK books are available at special discounts when purchased in bulk for sales
promotions, premiums, fund-raising, or education use. For details, contact:
DK Publishing Special Markets, 1745 Broadway, 20th Floor, New York, NY 10019
SpecialSales@dk.com

Printed and bound in China
www.dk.com
akidsco.com

MIX
Paper | Supporting
responsible forestry
FSC™ C018179

This book was made with Forest
Stewardship Council™ certified
paper – one small step in DK's
commitment to a sustainable future.
Learn more at www.dk.com/uk/
information/sustainability

For my dynamic, intelligent, imaginative, and inspiring son, Amari.

Amari's name is of African-Yoruba origins and means *strength*.

Intro
for grownups

Imagine if we'd been told as kids that strength is within every person and isn't limited to those with big muscles. Or that strength training helps us grow stronger mentally and physically instead of being taught the opposite... that it might stunt your growth!

This book aims to empower the minds of young people and inspire them to grow stronger with the understanding that strength is not about size or shape. Our goal is reframing strength from a limited perspective centered around vanity and expanding it for what it truly is: positivity.

This book gives universal and usable examples of how to start getting stronger as soon as today. Kids will learn that strength is about our hearts, minds, and willpower. Strength is for all people, of all ages, and all shapes and sizes.

Hey, I'm Sam. I'm a strength coach.

I LOVE helping people get

STRONGER!

Does that sound good to you?

Are you interested?

Are you ready?

Well, you might be thinking...

"HEY, SAM... I'M NOT AS STRONG AS MY FRIENDS."

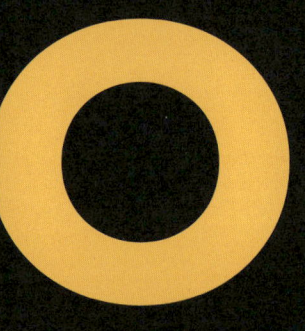

R "I'VE NEVER DONE THIS BEFORE, AND I DON'T KNOW IF I FEEL READY!"

But guess what?

NO ONE
EVER FEELS
TRULY READY.

My goal with this book is to provide you with tools and help you understand that fear is part of the process.

Conquering your fears is literally what strength is all about.

LET'S
TO

GET 💪 WORK!

Everyone has strength within them.

My strength has always been my ability to focus and push through challenges, even before I feel ready.

You are strong too, and I want
to help you practice and improve

YO

UR
STRENGTH.

A good place to start is understanding where your abilities are today and how they can improve tomorrow, and the next day, and the day after that.

It's about the big picture, not 1 single day, and the importance of sticking with it.

Because strength doesn't happen overnight—it happens little by little, over time.

Throughout my life, I've encountered many challenges:

getting sick,

getting hurt,

recovering from injuries,

my dad going far away from
home to serve in the military,

me going far away to
serve in the military,

being scared,

feeling alone,

and not being confident about
myself and my own abilities.

When challenges come my way,
I focus on consistently moving my
body and getting stronger from
the ground up and the inside out.

When I am scared,
I move my body.

When I feel alone,
I move my body.

When I am not feeling confident,
I move my body.

When I feel great,
I move my body.

And when I'm done, I always feel
better, happier, and energized.

The energy I gain from moving my body helps in every other thing I do.

I've also learned that **moving** my body is just as important as **resting** my body.

Rest can mean a few things:

Taking a break in between exercises.

Giving your body a day or 2 between workouts to get ready for your next one.

Actually resting, like taking a nap, or getting plenty of sleep at night.

And the most important
thing I've learned is this:

STRENGTH ISN'T ABOUT THE SIZE OF YOUR ARMS OR LEGS. IT'S ABOUT THE STRENGTH OF YOUR HEART AND MIND.

Here are a few ways to work on those muscles. (Yes, your heart and mind are muscles, too!)

Let's go all the way back to when you were a little baby.

When we are born, our bodies work really hard to learn new things like:

stretching,

moving our arms and legs,

lifting our heads,

holding our heads up,

and rolling over.

Those things may seem easy now, but building on those strengths is a great place to start.

The key to understanding how to get stronger is to know that new skills build upon what you already have.

So, wherever you are...

IS THE **RIGHT** PLACE TO START!

Here's an example:

How long can you stand on 1 foot?

How long can you raise your hand?

How long can you hold your breath?

Go ahead and try those out!

Now, how do we get stronger?

Can you do 1 of those things, for 1 second longer, for a whole week?

Then, 2 seconds longer the week after that?

This is

STRENGTH

TRAINING.

It may not be easy, but it is possible for everyone.

It doesn't matter how your body looks, or what age you are.

What matters is that you grow awareness of your

OWN

power and strength.

So, where do your heart
and mind come in?

THEY FUEL YOUR INNER STRENGTH!

Here's the deal: strength training can be hard.

It's mostly uncomfortable, yet extremely rewarding, because it helps you do things you never thought you could do.

When things get hard and your *mind* feels like it wants to stop—but you have the *heart* to keep going— you're using your inner strength.

And when I say your heart, I do mean your heart that moves blood and oxygen around your body.

But I also mean what makes you, you. (That is another definition for your **heart**.)

It's not about how you look,
or what you can do.

Strength is about adding a little bit over time, sticking with your goals, and, most importantly, not giving up.

EVE IN
OU!

Outro
for grownups

Grownups, there's a chance that when reading this book along with the kids in your life, some of these words have hit home for you too. It's important we all know that we are strong already.

By acknowledging that strength comes from within, we are able to feel empowered and ready to take action.

Start in small ways, like moving your body more often, meditating, or stretching for a few minutes daily.

And then, when you feel ready, work up to big ways, like moving small objects against gravity, pushing into slight discomfort while exercising, or taking time off to relax more frequently.

My hope is that you will refer to this book whenever challenges arise. No matter how difficult times may get, we are always able to find our way through by harnessing our inner strength.

About The Author

Sam Johnson (he/him) is a professional strength coach and entrepreneur who is passionate about leading people of all ages and backgrounds to live a healthy, purposeful, and sustainable lifestyle.

His 10+ years of coaching experience, as well as personally competing in the CrossFit Games, USA Weightlifting Nationals, and numerous sports help him to inspire sports athletes to reach their goals.

Sam's prior experience as a Staff Sergeant Combat Engineer in the United States Air Force gives him a unique perspective on strength when helping prospective military members train to be mentally and physically prepared for service. When he's not coaching, Sam loves to spend time with his wife and son, especially in the sun.

Made to empower.

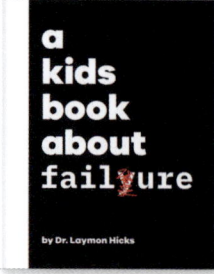

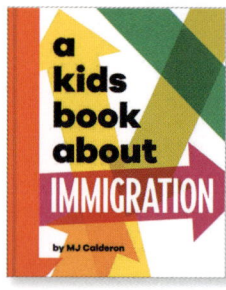

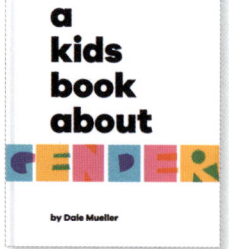
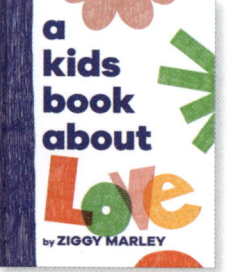
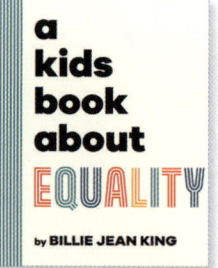

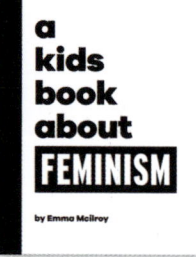

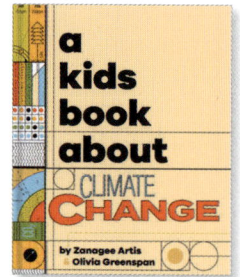

Discover more at akidsco.com